This book belongs to

Bella
Hippos Can Dance!

Shiko J

Bella Hippos Can Dance
Copyright @ 2020
by Blue Elephant Publishing

Published By Blue Elephant Publishing
ISBN #978-1-7357130-07

Written by Shiko J.

Illustrated by Bob Nagel

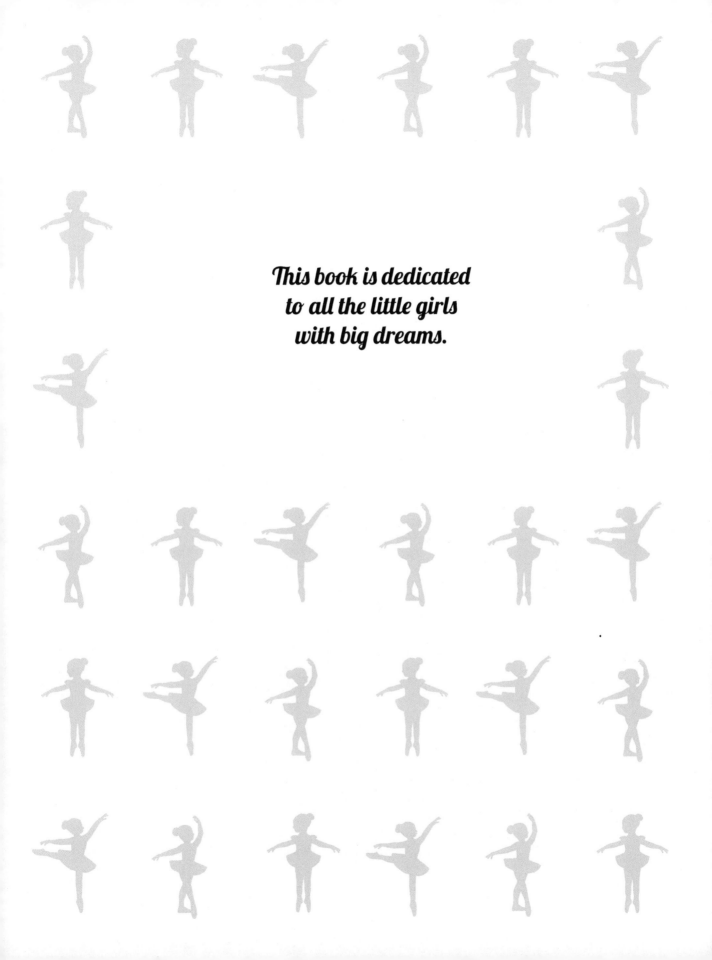

This book is dedicated
to all the little girls
with big dreams.

"Bella, Bella! Its time to get up for school," Mama screams.

Bella tumbles onto the floor with the sheets and pillows scattering across the room.

She giggles with excitement because today is sign-up day for the dance competition.

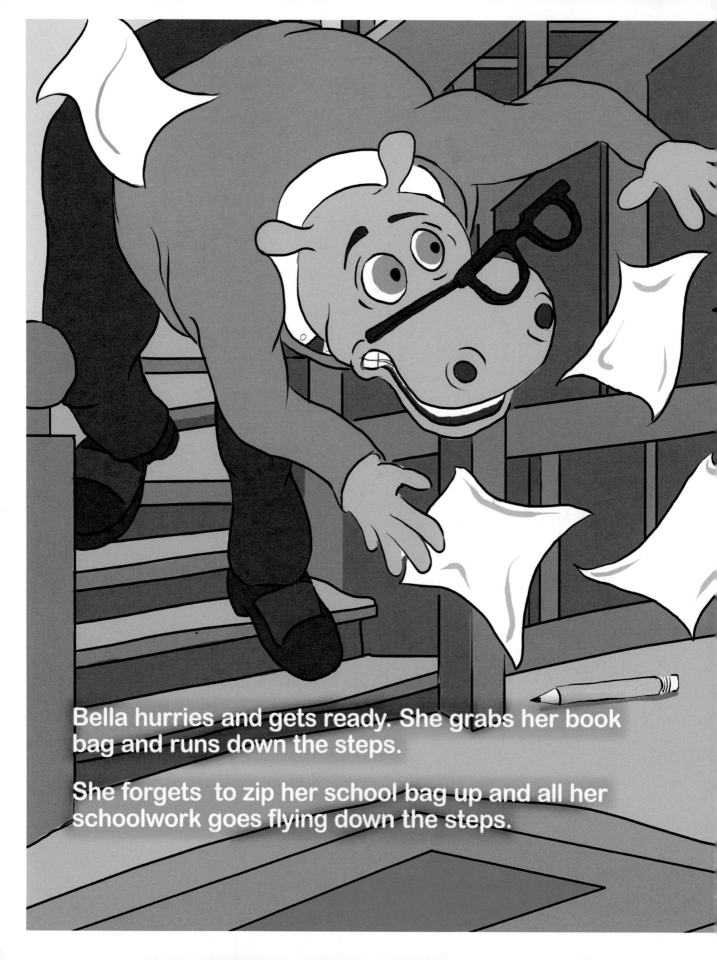

Bella hurries and gets ready. She grabs her book bag and runs down the steps.

She forgets to zip her school bag up and all her schoolwork goes flying down the steps.

"Don't worry Bella, go to the kitchen and I will bring your work," says Papa as he gathers the papers from the floor.

Excited, Bella runs to the kitchen!

She cannot wait to get to school today.

"Bella, eat your cereal," Mama says, "so you won't be late."

"I don't want to eat," Bella whines. "I am ready to get on the bus." "Mama, today is the big day to sign up for the dance competition," Bella eagerly tells her.

Bella takes a piece of toast that Mama hands her and runs towards the door.

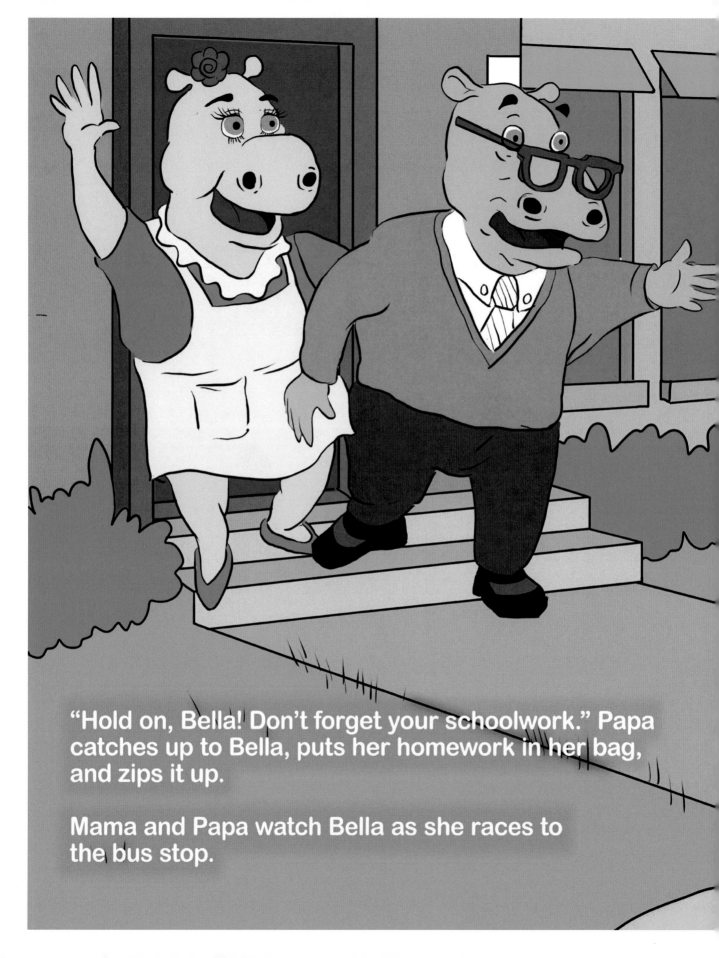

"Hold on, Bella! Don't forget your schoolwork." Papa catches up to Bella, puts her homework in her bag, and zips it up.

Mama and Papa watch Bella as she races to the bus stop.

They have worried looks on their faces because they both know that Bella has two left feet.

Bella runs to the bus stop to meet up with her two best friends, Lucy and Eva.

"Hey guys!" Bella shouts as she sees her friends.

"Hi Bella!" Lucy and Ava say at the same time and giggle.

"I am going to sign up for the dance competition today," Bella says as she cannot hold her excitement.

"You are?" says Eva.

"Are you?" Lucy says.

"I want to be the next, big ballerina!" Bella says as she begins to twist around almost hitting the garbage can.

"But Bella, you have never danced before!" Eva says.

"Ballet is hard!" Lucy says.

"Ms. Jones said that she would teach me," says Bella with confidence.

Eva and Lucy both worry. Everyone knows Bella has two left feet, and Hippos cannot dance.

Ringgggg! The third hour bell rings, and Bella bolts out to the signup sheet posted on the board outside the classroom.

"Excuse me, excuse me!" Bella says, as she pushes her way through the crowd.

She eagerly uses her pencil to write her name on the sheet.

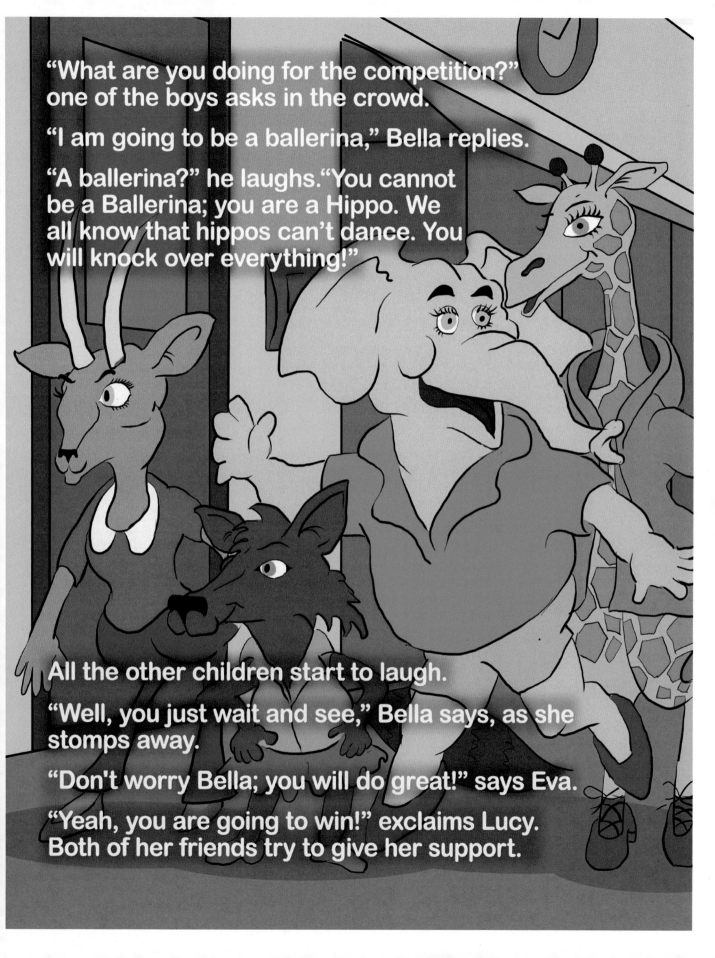

"What are you doing for the competition?" one of the boys asks in the crowd.

"I am going to be a ballerina," Bella replies.

"A ballerina?" he laughs. "You cannot be a Ballerina; you are a Hippo. We all know that hippos can't dance. You will knock over everything!"

All the other children start to laugh.

"Well, you just wait and see," Bella says, as she stomps away.

"Don't worry Bella; you will do great!" says Eva.

"Yeah, you are going to win!" exclaims Lucy. Both of her friends try to give her support.

After school, Bella goes straight to see Ms. Jones.

"Ms. Jones, Ms. Jones," Bella shouts as she runs in the gym.

"Hey, slow down!" Ms. Jones says, as Bella almost knocks over the ball rack. "What can I help you with, Bella?" Ms. Jones has a big smile on her face.

Ms. Jones, remember when you said that you would teach me ballet?" says Bella.

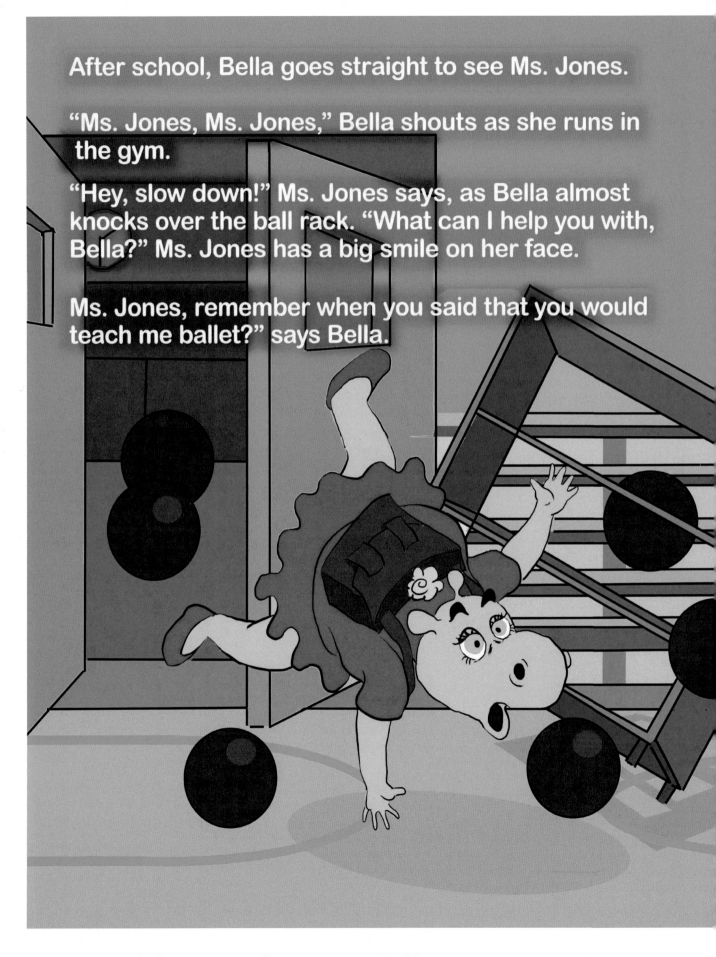

"Well yes, I do," Ms. Jones says. "I want to learn for the dancing competition!" exclaims Bella.

"You signed up? Good for you! When is the competition?" asks Ms. Jones.

"In two weeks," says Bella.

"Two weeks! That will not be enough time," Ms. Jones says. "The ballet takes time to learn, Bella." But the sad look on Bella's face makes Ms. Jones change her mind.

"This is what we shall do…every day after school, I will teach you a new step. It will not be easy, so you must practice, okay?"

"Yeah!" Bella cannot hold her happiness. "I promise, I will," Bella cheers. Bella jumps and twirls in the air like she already is a ballerina, all the way home.

The next day, Bella rises out of bed and does not even need the alarm clock or her mother. She is up and ready for school and ready for her first ballet practice. She rushes past her parents.

"Bella, here is your breakfast…" But before her mother gets it out, Bella grabs the toast off the plate and runs for the door.

"Oh, my! It seems like someone is in a rush to go to school today," Papa says as he looks up from his newspaper.

Bella cannot wait for the last bell to ring; she bolts out the door and into the Dance Hall.

"Great, Bella! You are here," says Ms. Jones. "Let us get started."

Bella tries to keep up with all the instructions that Ms. Jones is giving: "Point your toes, jump, twirl !" Ms. Jones shouts repeatedly.

"Phew!" This is hard Bella thought, as she falls a few times.

Some of the other children in the Dance Hall laugh. "Hahaha, Hippos can't dance."

Ms. Jones sees the look of discouragement on Bella's face, so she reminds her that it takes practice and Hippos can dance.

Bella gets up and tells herself "Hippos CAN dance!" Bella practices every day, nonstop!

Even though some laugh at her, she keeps going with her friends cheering her on.

She repeatedly tells herself that Hippos can dance.

The big day is here; Bella is scared and excited. She looks from behind the curtains of the stage and sees the whole school and her parents, sitting and waiting. She thinks about all those people watching her dance and gets scared.

"Bella, it's your turn" Ms. Jones says as she signals her on stage.

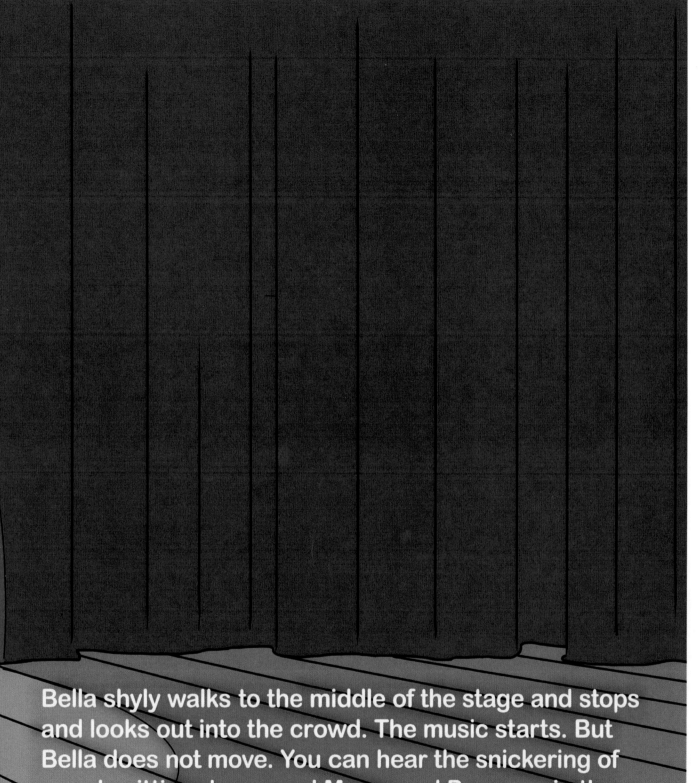

Bella shyly walks to the middle of the stage and stops and looks out into the crowd. The music starts. But Bella does not move. You can hear the snickering of people sitting down, and Mama and Papa are in the crowd. They look nervous.

"Bella, Bella," she hears Ms. Jones and her friends in the background calling to look over. Backstage, they have a poster that says, "HIPPOS CAN DANCE!"

Bella doesn't even realize when she starts moving, but she does the whole routine just as Ms. Jones had shown her.

When she stops, the whole hall is quiet. Soon after, everyone jumps up and down and cheers. "Bella, you did it!" Eva and Lucy cheer. "Hippos CAN dance!"

Made in the USA
Middletown, DE
04 May 2021